■ SCHOLAST

Week-by-Week Homework Packets

Spelling

Grade 1

by Kristin Geller

NEW YORK • TORONTO • LONDON • AUCKLAND • SYDNEY
MEXICO CITY • NEW DELHI • HONG KONG • BUENOS AIRES

Teaching *Resources*

Dedicated to two wonderful, inspiring, and caring first-grade colleagues,
Kim Newman and Sharon Manna.

Cover design by Lillian Kohli

Interior design by Sydney Wright

ISBN–13: 978-0-439-65096-0

ISBN–10: 0-439-65096-8

Copyright © 2007 by Kristin Geller

Published by Scholastic Inc.

All rights reserved.

Printed in the U.S.A

3 4 5 6 7 8 9 10   31   15 14 13 12 11

Contents

Spelling Lessons

Introduction

Dear First-Grade Teacher,

First grade is an amazing year! Nothing is more exciting than witnessing your students emerge as successful and independent readers and writers who enjoy literature and communicating.

One of the greatest challenges that first-grade teachers face is the individual pace at which students become independent readers and writers—some learn quickly while others require more practice. That's where *Week-by-Week Homework Packets: Spelling Grade 1* comes in. This effective spelling program can help students of varying abilities develop as writers and readers because it provides them with repeated opportunities to read and write essential vocabulary in a consistent and flexible manner. The weekly spelling lists are based on the Dolch High-Frequency Word List* and the 100 Highest-Frequency Writing Words List** and include 180 words that students will encounter with greatest frequency in their reading and writing during first grade. This program is mapped out from the beginning to the end of the school year and offers opportunities to differentiate each child's word list to ensure that the needs of all learners are met.

Plus, *Week-by-Week Homework Packets: Spelling Grade 1* is a snap to use. Simply copy three pages for every lesson—an assignment checklist and two pages of spelling activities—to send home with each child every Monday. Then, review the words in your classroom throughout the week. (See About This Book on pages 5–7 to find complete how-to's, management tips, and activity ideas.) On Friday, collect the homework and follow with a copy of Spell Check, the student assessment on page 10. Your students will be on their way to successful, independent reading and writing before you know it!

Enjoy—and here's to super spellers!

Sincerely,

Kristin Geller

---

*Dolch High-Frequency Word List—a list of 220 words compiled by E.W. Dolch in 1936. These words are generally referred to as Sight Words, High-Frequency Words, or Dolch Words, and can make up 75% of the reading material that students encounter.

**100 Highest-Frequency Writing Words List—developed by Rebecca Sitton, cited by Judy Lynch in *Word Learning, Word Making, Word Sorting: 50 Lessons for Success* (Scholastic, 2002)

About This Book

Week-by-Week Homework Packets: Spelling Grade 1 includes 36 weeks of word lists and activities for use throughout the school year. See below for a close-up look at the program's components as well as ideas to help you get the most out of this valuable resource.

Weekly Spelling Lesson Program Components

Weekly Spelling Lesson Packets

The weekly homework packets (pages 12–72) consist of the following three pages:

1. The Weekly Spelling Work Checklist (page 12) lists the homework to be completed each night of the week and asks for a parent signature.

2. The first page of each packet includes a word list, a word-writing activity, and an alphabetical ordering activity.

3. The second page includes a word box activity, a sentence completion activity, and a bonus section.

Simply copy each page, staple together to form a packet, and distribute to students every week to take home and complete.

Weekly Spell Check Assessments

Conduct a Spell Check, the student assessment on page 10 at the end of a week-long study of a word list to assess each student's mastery. This assessment should be administered in a simple, stress-free way that will allow students to demonstrate their competency. After grading, record the information on the Teacher Spell Check Assessment grid (page 11) to track each student's progress. The information you gain from these assessments will help target your differentiation of each child's weekly word list.

Review Lesson Packets

Review Lessons A–F (pages 73–80) will provide students with further practice spelling all 30 words introduced over a five-week period. Review Lesson A includes words from Lessons 1 through 5, Review Lesson B includes words from Lessons 6 through 10, and so on. (See page 9 for a list of all 180 spelling words.) The review lessons consist of the following three pages:

1. The Review Spelling Work Checklist (page 73) lists the homework to be completed each night of the week and asks for a parent signature.

2. The first page of each review packet (pages 74-79) includes a word search, a word scramble, and a review word list.

3. The second page (page 80) includes an activity in which students create five original sentences.

Simply copy each page, staple together to form a packet, and distribute to students during a review week to take home and complete. (The review lessons are not intended to be followed by a Spell Check assessment.)

> ## Home-School Connection
>
> ### Start of the School Year
>
> Involving family members is a wonderful way to incorporate the spelling packets into your classroom and your students' lives. At the start of school, send home a copy of the Family Letter (page 8) which explains the program and describes the expectations for the year. Consider also sending home a copy of the weekly Spell Check, the student assessment on page 10 to give families an idea of the manner in which students will be assessed.

Introducing the Spelling Words

As new spelling words are introduced each week, take the time to discuss each word individually. You might speak it, read it, and spell it; define it and use it in a sentence; or develop phonemic awareness by playing sound matching games. For example, while using the homework packet that contains Lesson 4 (page 19) you might select the spelling word *at* and ask students to find other words that have the same beginning sound, such as *apple* or *acrobat*, or the same ending sound, such as *pit* or *hut*. Then, consider adding the new list of spelling words to your classroom word wall. It is important for students to have an introduction to each list of words before working on the homework packet.

Tips for Management & Differentiated Learning

There are a variety of ways to manage this spelling program in your classroom. I've found that using folders or binders is an effective way to organize each child's work. Every week, provide students with a copy of the spelling words to add to their folders/binders. Soon they will have a handy resource of words that they can reference when working on writing tasks! These folders/binders can be kept within each student's desk or in a private work area. Because all students will be working off of the same basic word list, a consistent program is established—but there is also flexibility. The Class Words and My Words sections of the word list present opportunities for differentiation.

- Class Words provide the opportunity to incorporate words from other areas of your curriculum. For example, if your class is studying pond life, words such as *pond*, *tadpole*, and *lily pad* might be included here.

- My Words provide the opportunity to reinforce or enrich individual word lists. Students who are ready for increased difficulty can add challenging words to this section, while those who require further reinforcement can include troublesome words until mastered. For example, if a student spells *people* incorrectly on a Spell Check, he or she can add it to this section the following week.

Extending Learning

Integrate the weekly word lists throughout the school day. Suggestions follow.

Learning Centers

- Word Work Center—Students can complete activities such as stamping the words with letter stamps, writing the words on write-on/wipe-off boards, building the words with magnetic letters and boards, or using the words to write short stories.

- Game Center—Students can play games with the words such as BINGO, Spelling Word Match (similar to the card game Concentration), and Word War (similar to the card game War). Each of these activities requires the creation of game boards and/or word cards, but are well worth the effort.

- Read & Write Center—Students can have fun reviewing the spelling words on the word wall using materials such as fun pointers and pretend reading glasses, or a clipboard and markers, pens, or other appealing writing utensils.

Morning Message

A wonderful way to start each day is to write a morning message that incorporates both the weekly spelling words and a shared writing activity. During this interactive writing exercise students can circle or highlight spelling words, fill in missing letters, words, and/or phrases, and correct mistakes, all while learning the important skills of sentence structure, comprehension, phonics, and punctuation. See below for a sample message.

> G_ _d morn_ _ _! Today is _uesday, _eptember _ _, _ _ _ _.
>
> dO _ _ _ ha_e a _avoRite fOod _ _ _ _ you like to eat?
>
> What _ _ it? Did YoU bring it _ _ _ snack?

(This sample message contains some of the spelling words from Lesson 2 on page 15—*it, of, for, in, is, that*.)

Dictation Journal

To provide students with opportunities to use spelling words in meaningful ways, and to help assess their understanding, consider using dictation journals with your class. These are used on a weekly basis and can be created with any journal or notebook, or by stapling blank sheets of paper together to form a journal. Begin by dictating a sentence that contains a spelling word. For example, while using the homework packet that contains Lesson 16 (page 43) you might dictate the following sentence: *I love a cold drink of water.* Then ask students to underline the spelling word (*water*). After dictating five more sentences—one for each of the remaining spelling words—review the sentences as a class to correct for spelling and grammar. The journals can also be used for students to create lists of words that share similarities with their spelling words. Students might list words that rhyme or words with the same beginning or ending sound. And students especially love when a timer is set to create a word list race!

Dear Family,

In our classroom, your child is learning about language—speaking, listening, reading, writing, and spelling. Our spelling program assists students in their discovery of language. The first-grade spelling words are comprised of high-frequency words. These are words that students will read, write, and speak constantly, so accurate spelling is important!

Each week your child will bring home a packet that includes a list of spelling words and homework activities. The words and activities will be introduced and reviewed in class, but your child may need further assistance learning to spell the words and completing the activities. The homework packet is due each Friday and will be followed by a Spell Check to assess your child's mastery of the week's words.

You will notice that your child may have additional words in the Class Words or My Words sections of the word list. Class Words are words that we are studying or focusing on as part of a unit of study in our classroom. My Words are words used to differentiate spelling instruction for every student. They are words used to reinforce or enrich your child's individual spelling program.

Thank you for your support in building super spellers!

Sincerely,

Spelling Lesson Sequence

Lesson 1- the, and, to, I, you, a
Lesson 2- is, that, for, it, of, in
Lesson 3- was, on, are, as, he, she
Lesson 4- they, at, with, his, be, her
Lesson 5- from, or, by, one, have, but
Review Lesson A

Lesson 6- go, all, had, what, no, this
Lesson 7- when, we, can, your, me, not
Lesson 8- there, an, my, said, which, if
Lesson 9- how, will, each, like, them, up
Lesson 10- make, about, were, him, good, do
Review Lesson B

Lesson 11- out, then, some, two, their, many
Lesson 12- so, has, would, other, these, into
Lesson 13- could, more, see, than, time, been
Lesson 14- way, look, who, now, first, people
Lesson 15- find, three, did, down, under, use
Review Lesson C

Lesson 16- only, day, made, water, may, get
Lesson 17- because, long, call, man, over, woman
Lesson 18- again, thing, here, say, come, after
Lesson 19- going, back, walk, part, done, stop
Lesson 20- best, know, think, must, very, just
Review Lesson D

Lesson 21- where, little, most, away, thank, right
Lesson 22- children, much, never, why, put, tall
Lesson 23- birthday, does, left, give, short, far
Lesson 24- hot, cold, warm, cool, wet, dry
Lesson 25- mother, father, brother, sister, girl, boy
Review Lesson E

Lesson 26- farm, grass, flower, house, school, garden
Lesson 27- cat, dog, cow, duck, horse, frog
Lesson 28- rabbit, pig, bird, sheep, fish, goat
Lesson 29- red, blue, yellow, green, purple, color
Lesson 30- white, black, brown, pink, gray, orange
Review Lesson F

Name _____   Lesson _____

Date _____

Spell Check

1. _____

2. _____

3. _____

4. _____

5. _____

6. _____

7. _____

8. _____

9. _____

10. _____

My Spell Check Score: ☐

10

Week-by-Week Homework Packets: Spelling Grade 1 Scholastic Teaching Resources Student Spell Check Assessment

Teacher Spell Check Assessment

Teacher _____

Grade _____ Year _____

Student	Lesson 1	Lesson 2	Lesson 3	Lesson 4	Lesson 5	Lesson 6	Lesson 7	Lesson 8	Lesson 9	Lesson 10	Lesson 11	Lesson 12	Lesson 13	Lesson 14	Lesson 15	Lesson 16	Lesson 17	Lesson 18	Lesson 19	Lesson 20	Lesson 21	Lesson 22	Lesson 23	Lesson 24	Lesson 25	Lesson 26	Lesson 27	Lesson 28	Lesson 29	Lesson 30

Name _____

WEEKLY
Spelling Work

☐ **Monday**   Words: Read your words and write each word three times.

☐ **Tuesday**   ABC Order: Write your words in alphabetical order.

☐ **Wednesday** Word Boxes: Write your spelling words in the correct word boxes.

☐ **Thursday**   Sentences: Read the sentences and fill in your missing spelling words.

☐ **Friday**   Return this homework and be ready for Spell Check!

Parent Signature _____

☐ **BONUS**   Write two sentences. In each sentence use at least one word from any of your three word lists. Then underline the word(s) in each sentence.

Week-by-Week Homework Packets: Spelling Grade 1 Scholastic Teaching Resources

Name _____

Spelling Words	Class Words	My Words
the I and you to a		

Words

1. _____

   _____

   _____

2. _____

   _____

   _____

3. _____

   _____

   _____

4. _____

   _____

   _____

5. _____

   _____

6. _____

   _____

   _____

7. _____

   _____

   _____

8. _____

   _____

   _____

9. _____

   _____

   _____

10. _____

   _____

   _____

A B C Order

1. _____

2. _____

3. _____

4. _____

5. _____

6. _____

7. _____

8. _____

9. _____

10. _____

Word Boxes

 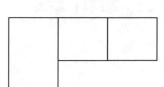 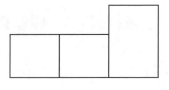

 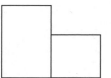 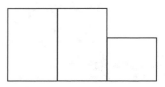

Sentences

1. The boy _____ girl can jump.

2. Put _____ toy in the box.

3. Do you have _____ pet?

4. I am going _____ have fun.

5. _____ love to ride my bike with my sister.

6. Do _____ have a favorite ice cream flavor?

Bonus

1. _____

_____

2. _____

_____

14

Name _____

Spelling Words	Class Words	My Words
it in		
of is		
for that		

Words

1. _____

   _____

   _____

2. _____

   _____

   _____

3. _____

   _____

   _____

4. _____

   _____

5. _____

   _____

6. _____

   _____

   _____

7. _____

   _____

   _____

8. _____

   _____

   _____

9. _____

   _____

10. _____

    _____

A B C Order

1. _____

2. _____

3. _____

4. _____

5. _____

6. _____

7. _____

8. _____

9. _____

10. _____

Word Boxes

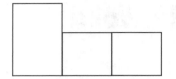 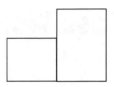 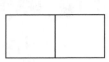

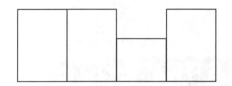  

Sentences

1. What _____ your name?

2. Where did you get _____ book?

3. I can do _____!

4. He is a friend _____ mine.

5. The cat can go _____ the house.

6. Did you pay _____ the candy?

Bonus

1. _____

_____

2. _____

_____

Week-by-Week Homework Packets: Spelling Grade 1 Scholastic Teaching Resources

Name _____

Spelling Words | Class Words | My Words

Spelling Words		Class Words	My Words
on	was		
are	he		
as	she		

Words

1. _____

_____

_____

2. _____

_____

_____

3. _____

_____

_____

4. _____

_____

_____

5. _____

_____

6. _____

_____

_____

7. _____

_____

_____

8. _____

_____

_____

9. _____

_____

_____

10. _____

_____

ABC Order

1. _____

2. _____

3. _____

4. _____

5. _____

6. _____

7. _____

8. _____

9. _____

10. _____

Word Boxes

Lesson 3 continued

Word Boxes

Sentences

1. He _____ at his friend's house yesterday.

2. Can you hop _____ one foot?

3. The girl sat up so _____ could see better.

4. They _____ my friends.

5. _____ is my big brother.

6. The bunny is as soft _____ silk.

Bonus

1. _____

_____

2. _____

_____

18

Week-by-Week Homework Packets: Spelling Grade 1 Scholastic Teaching Resources

Name _____

Spelling Words	Class Words	My Words
with at his be they her		

Words

1. _____

   _____

   _____

2. _____

   _____

   _____

3. _____

   _____

   _____

4. _____

   _____

   _____

5. _____

   _____

6. _____

   _____

   _____

7. _____

   _____

   _____

8. _____

   _____

   _____

9. _____

   _____

10. _____

   _____

A B C Order

1. _____

2. _____

3. _____

4. _____

5. _____

6. _____

7. _____

8. _____

9. _____

10. _____

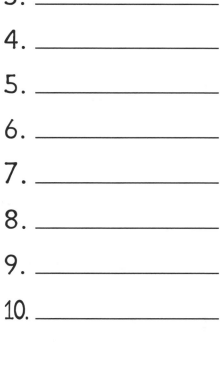

Word Boxes

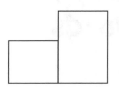 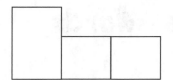 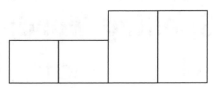

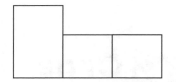 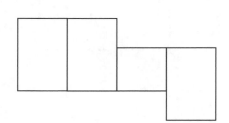 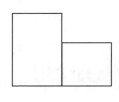

Sentences

1. My sister and _____ friend are funny!

2. We will _____ home soon.

3. My dad will meet me _____ the store.

4. _____ are very good friends.

5. She went to the store _____ her mom.

6. He read a book with _____ teacher.

Bonus

1. _____

   _____

2. _____

   _____

Week-by-Week Homework Packets: Spelling Grade 1 Scholastic Teaching Resources

Name _____

Spelling Words	Class Words	My Words
from one		
or have		
by but		

Words

1. _____
   _____
   _____

2. _____
   _____
   _____

3. _____
   _____
   _____

4. _____
   _____
   _____

5. _____
   _____

6. _____
   _____

7. _____
   _____

8. _____
   _____

9. _____
   _____

10. _____
   _____

ABC Order

1. _____
2. _____
3. _____
4. _____
5. _____
6. _____
7. _____
8. _____
9. _____
10. _____

Word Boxes

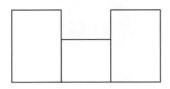
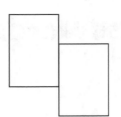
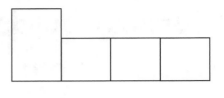

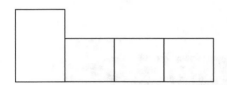
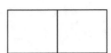
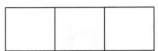

Sentences

1. I have three fish but only _____ cat.

2. My mom drives her car home _____ work.

3. Is his coat black _____ blue?

4. The book was written _____ my favorite author.

5. We went outside _____ then it started to rain.

6. Do you _____ a brother?

Bonus

1. _____

_____

2. _____

_____

Week-by-Week Homework Packets: Spelling Grade 1 Scholastic Teaching Resources

Name _____

Spelling Words		Class Words	My Words
all	had		
what	this		
no	go		

Words

1. _____
   _____
   _____

2. _____
   _____
   _____

3. _____
   _____

4. _____
   _____
   _____

5. _____
   _____

6. _____
   _____

7. _____
   _____

8. _____
   _____

9. _____

10. _____

A B C Order

1. _____
2. _____
3. _____
4. _____
5. _____
6. _____
7. _____
8. _____
9. _____
10. _____

Word Boxes

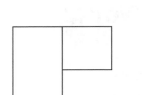
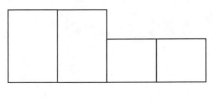
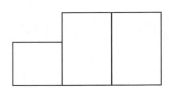

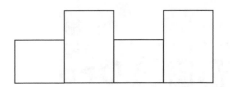
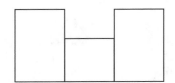
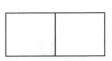

Sentences

1. _____ color is your dress?

2. Please clean up _____ of your toys!

3. I like to _____ to the park.

4. Can you help me read _____ book?

5. There is _____ school today!

6. Yesterday I _____ cake after dinner.

Bonus

1. _____

_____

2. _____

_____

24

Name _____

Spelling Words	Class Words	My Words
when your we me can not		

Words

1. _____

_____

_____

2. _____

_____

_____

3. _____

_____

_____

4. _____

_____

_____

5. _____

_____

_____

6. _____

_____

_____

7. _____

_____

_____

8. _____

_____

_____

9. _____

_____

_____

10. _____

_____

_____

A B C Order

1. _____

2. _____

3. _____

4. _____

5. _____

6. _____

7. _____

8. _____

9. _____

10. _____

Word Boxes

Sentences

1. Is that _____ backpack?

2. My brother is older than _____.

3. She _____ ride her bike very fast.

4. I am _____ going to the party.

5. _____ do we go to recess?

6. _____ like our new neighbors.

Bonus

1. _____

   _____

2. _____

   _____

Week-by-Week Homework Packets: Spelling Grade 1 Scholastic Teaching Resources

Name _____

Spelling Words	Class Words	My Words
there an said if which my		

Words

1. _____
   _____
   _____

2. _____
   _____
   _____

3. _____
   _____
   _____

4. _____
   _____
   _____

5. _____
   _____

6. _____
   _____
   _____

7. _____
   _____
   _____

8. _____
   _____
   _____

9. _____
   _____
   _____

10. _____
    _____

ABC Order

1. _____
2. _____
3. _____
4. _____
5. _____
6. _____
7. _____
8. _____
9. _____
10. _____

Word Boxes

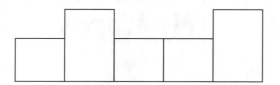 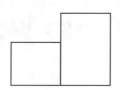 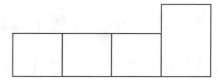

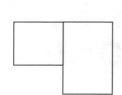 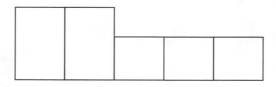 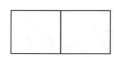

Sentences

1. "Time for bed," _____ our dad.

2. _____ ice cream is your favorite?

3. She wore _____ coat instead of hers!

4. Ask your mom _____ you can come to my house.

5. He eats _____ apple every day.

6. Did you see the big dog over _____ ?

Bonus

1. _____

_____

2. _____

_____

Week-by-Week Homework Packets: Spelling Grade 1 Scholastic Teaching Resources

Name _____

Spelling Words

will	them
up	each
like	how

Class Words

My Words

Words

1. _____
   _____
   _____

2. _____
   _____
   _____

3. _____
   _____
   _____

4. _____
   _____
   _____

5. _____
   _____

6. _____
   _____
   _____

7. _____
   _____
   _____

8. _____
   _____
   _____

9. _____
   _____

10. _____
   _____

A B C Order

1. _____
2. _____
3. _____
4. _____
5. _____
6. _____
7. _____
8. _____
9. _____
10. _____

Word Boxes

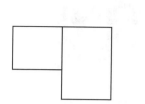 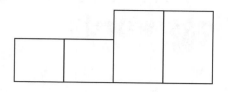 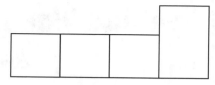

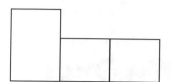 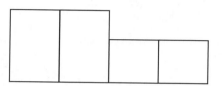 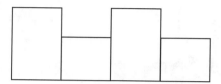

Sentences

1. _____ student gets two pencils.

2. They _____ to play soccer.

3. Who _____ bring me to school?

4. I had dinner with _____ last night.

5. The plane went high _____ into the sky.

6. _____ many desks do we have?

Bonus

1. _____

_____

2. _____

_____

Week-by-Week Homework Packets: Spelling Grade 1 Scholastic Teaching Resources

Name _____

Spelling Words	Class Words	My Words
make good		
were do		
about him		

Words

1. _____

_____

_____

2. _____

_____

_____

3. _____

_____

_____

4. _____

_____

_____

5. _____

_____

6. _____

_____

_____

7. _____

_____

_____

8. _____

_____

_____

9. _____

_____

_____

10. _____

_____

ABC Order

1. _____
2. _____
3. _____
4. _____
5. _____
6. _____
7. _____
8. _____
9. _____
10. _____

Word Boxes

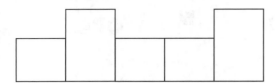 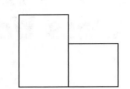 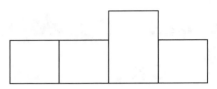

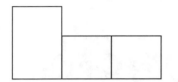  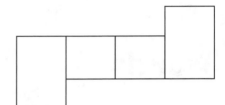

Sentences

1. _____ you like to play outside?

2. The book was _____ a silly clown.

3. This apple pie tastes _____!

4. _____ you at school yesterday?

5. I walked home with _____ and his brother.

6. Did you help _____ this cake?

Bonus

1. _____

_____

2. _____

_____

Week-by-Week Homework Packets: Spelling Grade 1 Scholastic Teaching Resources

Name _____

Spelling Words	Class Words	My Words
out two then their some many		

Words

1. _____

_____

_____

2. _____

_____

_____

3. _____

_____

_____

4. _____

_____

_____

5. _____

_____

6. _____

_____

_____

7. _____

_____

_____

8. _____

_____

_____

9. _____

_____

_____

10. _____

_____

A B C Order

1. _____

2. _____

3. _____

4. _____

5. _____

6. _____

7. _____

8. _____

9. _____

10. _____

Word Boxes

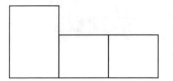
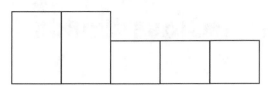
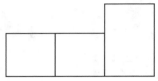

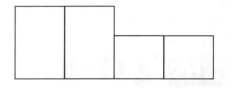
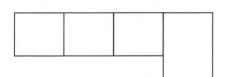
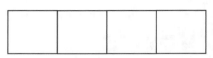

Sentences

1. How _____ pets do you have?

2. Let's go _____ and play!

3. We ate dinner _____ had dessert.

4. Would you like _____ candy?

5. Now we have _____ cats.

6. _____ toys are more fun than mine!

Bonus

1. _____

_____

2. _____

_____

Week-by-Week Homework Packets: Spelling Grade 1 Scholastic Teaching Resources

Name _____

Spelling Words

into   so
would   has
other   these

Class Words

My Words

Words

1. _____

   _____

   _____

2. _____

   _____

   _____

3. _____

   _____

   _____

4. _____

   _____

   _____

5. _____

   _____

6. _____

   _____

   _____

7. _____

   _____

   _____

8. _____

   _____

   _____

9. _____

   _____

10. _____

    _____

ABC Order

1. _____

2. _____

3. _____

4. _____

5. _____

6. _____

7. _____

8. _____

9. _____

10. _____

Word Boxes

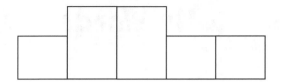

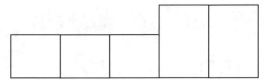

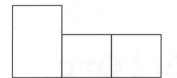
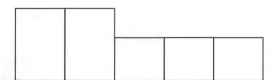
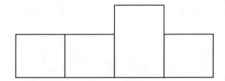

Sentences

1. She _____ three cousins.

2. Let's go the _____ way.

3. _____ pancakes taste great!

4. I _____ love a red lollipop.

5. The mouse went _____ the hole in the wall.

6. The kitten has grown _____ big!

Bonus

1. _____

    _____

2. _____

    _____

Week-by-Week Homework Packets: Spelling Grade 1 Scholastic Teaching Resources

Name _____

Spelling Words

could	than
more	been
see	time

Class Words

My Words

Words

1. _____
   _____
   _____

2. _____
   _____
   _____

3. _____
   _____
   _____

4. _____
   _____
   _____

5. _____
   _____

6. _____
   _____
   _____

7. _____
   _____
   _____

8. _____
   _____
   _____

9. _____
   _____
   _____

10. _____
    _____

A B C Order

1. _____
2. _____
3. _____
4. _____
5. _____
6. _____
7. _____
8. _____
9. _____
10. _____

Word Boxes

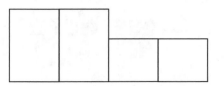
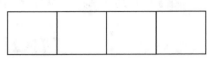

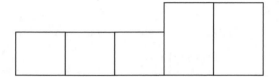

Sentences

1. Do you want _____ pizza?

2. The twins _____ not come to my party.

3. What _____ does the show start?

4. I like pie better _____ cake.

5. Can you _____ the screen?

6. Where have you _____?

Bonus

1. _____

   _____

2. _____

   _____

Week-by-Week Homework Packets: Spelling Grade 1 Scholastic Teaching Resources

Name _____

Spelling Words

first	way
people	who
now	look

Class Words

My Words

Words

1. _____
   _____
   _____

2. _____
   _____
   _____

3. _____
   _____
   _____

4. _____
   _____

5. _____
   _____

6. _____
   _____
   _____

7. _____
   _____
   _____

8. _____
   _____
   _____

9. _____
   _____

10. _____
    _____

A B C Order

1. _____
2. _____
3. _____
4. _____
5. _____
6. _____
7. _____
8. _____
9. _____
10. _____

Word Boxes

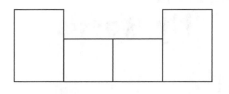 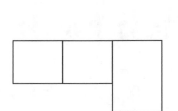 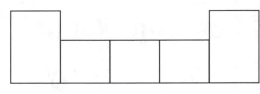

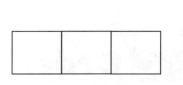 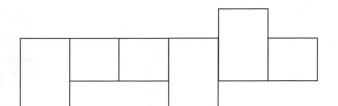 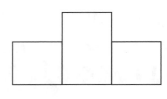

Sentences

1. _____ is on the phone?

2. You two _____ alike!

3. Sam can't play right _____.

4. There were a lot of _____ at the store.

5. She was the _____ to finish the race!

6. Which _____ did he go?

Bonus

1. _____

_____

2. _____

_____

Name _____

Spelling Words		Class Words	My Words
three	did		
under	use		
down	find		

Words

1. _____

_____

_____

2. _____

_____

_____

3. _____

_____

_____

4. _____

_____

_____

5. _____

_____

6. _____

_____

_____

7. _____

_____

_____

8. _____

_____

_____

9. _____

_____

_____

10. _____

_____

A B C Order

1. _____

2. _____

3. _____

4. _____

5. _____

6. _____

7. _____

8. _____

9. _____

10. _____

Word Boxes

 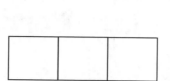 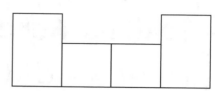

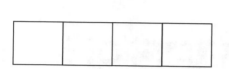 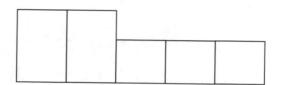 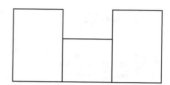

Sentences

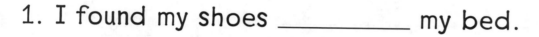

1. I found my shoes _____ my bed.

2. He fell _____ and hurt his leg.

3. Please _____ a smock when you paint.

4. _____ you see the rain last night?

5. I can't _____ my favorite backpack!

6. They have _____ turtles.

Bonus

1. _____

   _____

2. _____

   _____

Week-by-Week Homework Packets: Spelling Grade 1 Scholastic Teaching Resources

Name _____

Spelling Words		**Class Words**	**My Words**
made	get		
water	day		
only	may		

Words

1. _____

_____

_____

2. _____

_____

_____

3. _____

_____

_____

4. _____

_____

_____

5. _____

_____

6. _____

_____

_____

7. _____

_____

_____

8. _____

_____

_____

9. _____

_____

10. _____

_____

ABC Order

1. _____
2. _____
3. _____
4. _____
5. _____
6. _____
7. _____
8. _____
9. _____
10. _____

Word Boxes

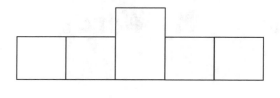 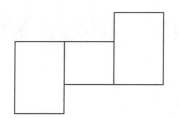 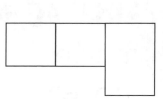

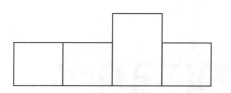 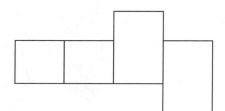 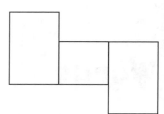

Sentences

1. There are _____ four days of school left.

2. Would you like a drink of _____?

3. I _____ a gift for my grandmother.

4. I hope we will _____ a puppy.

5. My birthday is my favorite _____ of the year!

6. She _____ need to go home first.

Bonus

1. _____

   _____

2. _____

   _____

Week-by-Week Homework Packets: Spelling Grade 1 Scholastic Teaching Resources

Name _____

Spelling Words	Class Words	My Words
call long		
woman man		
because over		

Words

1. _____

   _____

   _____

2. _____

   _____

   _____

3. _____

   _____

   _____

4. _____

   _____

   _____

5. _____

   _____

6. _____

   _____

   _____

7. _____

   _____

   _____

8. _____

   _____

   _____

9. _____

   _____

   _____

10. _____

   _____

A B C Order

1. _____

2. _____

3. _____

4. _____

5. _____

6. _____

7. _____

8. _____

9. _____

10. _____

Word Boxes

Sentences

1. She has a cast _____ she broke her arm.

2. The _____ helped me so I thanked her.

3. Did you _____ my name?

4. Your hair has grown so _____!

5. I jumped _____ the log.

6. He is a tall _____.

Bonus

1. _____

_____

2. _____

_____

Week-by-Week Homework Packets: Spelling Grade 1 Scholastic Teaching Resources

Name _____

Spelling Words	Class Words	My Words
again say		
thing come		
here after		

Words

1. _____
   _____
   _____

2. _____
   _____
   _____

3. _____
   _____
   _____

4. _____
   _____
   _____

5. _____
   _____

6. _____
   _____
   _____

7. _____
   _____
   _____

8. _____
   _____
   _____

9. _____
   _____
   _____

10. _____
    _____

A B C Order

1. _____
2. _____
3. _____
4. _____
5. _____
6. _____
7. _____
8. _____
9. _____
10. _____

Word Boxes

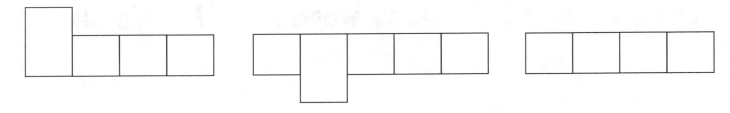

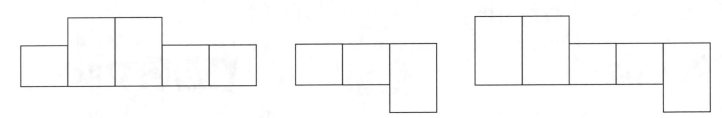

Sentences

1. What did you _____?

2. Can you come to my house _____ school?

3. That is the funniest _____ I've ever heard!

4. Do you want to play the game _____?

5. "_____ it is," I shouted.

6. Would you like to _____ to my party?

Bonus

1. _____

   _____

2. _____

   _____

Name _____

Spelling Words

going	done
back	stop
part	walk

Class Words

My Words

Words

1. _____
_____
_____

2. _____
_____
_____

3. _____
_____
_____

4. _____
_____
_____

5. _____
_____
_____

6. _____
_____
_____

7. _____
_____
_____

8. _____
_____
_____

9. _____
_____
_____

10. _____
_____
_____

ABC Order

1. _____
2. _____
3. _____
4. _____
5. _____
6. _____
7. _____
8. _____
9. _____
10. _____

Word Boxes

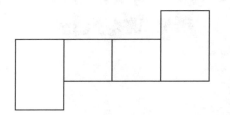 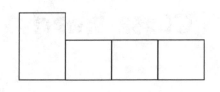 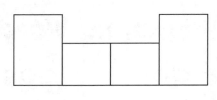

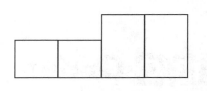 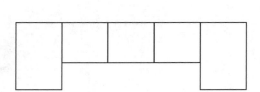 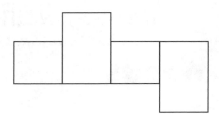

Sentences

1. He put the puzzle pieces _____ in the box.

2. Please _____ shouting!

3. We are _____ on vacation in two weeks.

4. Which _____ of the story did you like best?

5. They went for a _____ after dinner.

6. I am _____ with all of my homework.

Bonus

1. _____

   _____

2. _____

   _____

Week-by-Week Homework Packets: Spelling Grade 1 Scholastic Teaching Resources

Name _____

Spelling Words		Class Words	My Words
best	must		
know	very		
think	just		

Words

1. _____
_____
_____

2. _____
_____
_____

3. _____
_____
_____

4. _____
_____
_____

5. _____
_____

6. _____
_____
_____

7. _____
_____
_____

8. _____
_____
_____

9. _____
_____
_____

10. _____
_____

ABC Order

1. _____
2. _____
3. _____
4. _____
5. _____
6. _____
7. _____
8. _____
9. _____
10. _____

Word Boxes

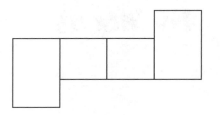
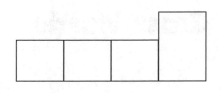
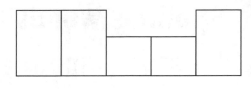

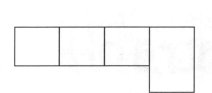
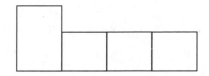
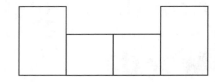

Sentences

1. I _____ today is a good day for ice skating.

2. He likes writing _____.

3. My mom said that I _____ clean my room!

4. Do you _____ the answer?

5. The man _____ smiled and waved.

6. It is getting _____ cold outside!

Bonus

1. _____

   _____

2. _____

   _____

Week-by-Week Homework Packets: Spelling Grade 1 Scholastic Teaching Resources

Name _____

Spelling Words	Class Words	My Words
little right where most thank away		

Words

1. _____

_____

_____

2. _____

_____

_____

3. _____

_____

_____

4. _____

_____

_____

5. _____

_____

6. _____

_____

_____

7. _____

_____

_____

8. _____

_____

9. _____

_____

_____

10. _____

_____

A B C Order

1. _____

2. _____

3. _____

4. _____

5. _____

6. _____

7. _____

8. _____

9. _____

10. _____

Word Boxes

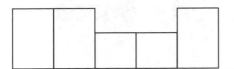 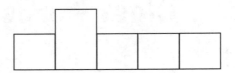 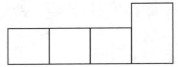

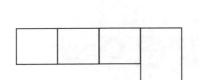 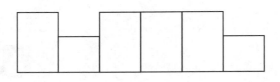 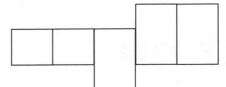

Sentences

1. Turn _____ at the stop sign.

2. _____ you for the great gift.

3. The puppy is so _____.

4. _____ did you go after school?

5. Please put your toys _____.

6. I ate _____ of my dinner.

Bonus

1. _____

   _____

2. _____

   _____

Name _____

Spelling Words

never	put
children	tall
much	why

Class Words

My Words

Words

1. _____

_____

_____

2. _____

_____

_____

3. _____

_____

_____

4. _____

_____

_____

5. _____

_____

6. _____

_____

_____

7. _____

_____

_____

8. _____

_____

_____

9. _____

_____

_____

10. _____

_____

ABC Order

1. _____

2. _____

3. _____

4. _____

5. _____

6. _____

7. _____

8. _____

9. _____

10. _____

Word Boxes

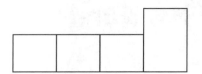 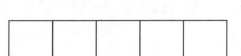 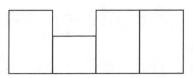

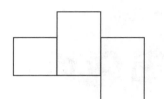 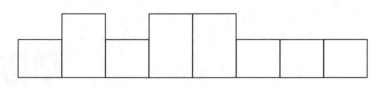 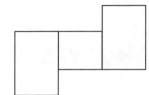

Sentences

1. There are many _____ in my class.

2. What a _____ tree!

3. Please _____ the plates on the table.

4. How _____ money do we have left?

5. I have _____ been to Canada.

6. _____ did you do that?

Bonus

1. _____

    _____

2. _____

    _____

Week-by-Week Homework Packets: Spelling Grade 1   Scholastic Teaching Resources

Name _____

Spelling Words	Class Words	My Words
birthday far		
does left		
short give		

Words

1. _____

_____

_____

2. _____

_____

_____

3. _____

_____

_____

4. _____

_____

_____

5. _____

_____

6. _____

_____

_____

7. _____

_____

_____

8. _____

_____

_____

9. _____

_____

_____

10. _____

_____

ABC Order

1. _____

2. _____

3. _____

4. _____

5. _____

6. _____

7. _____

8. _____

9. _____

10. _____

Word Boxes

Sentences

1. Our grandparents live _____ away.

2. There aren't any cookies _____.

3. I get a _____ haircut when it is warm.

4. My _____ is in March.

5. Please _____ this letter to your teacher.

6. _____ your friend want to play?

Bonus

1. _____

   _____

2. _____

   _____

Week-by-Week Homework Packets: Spelling Grade 1 Scholastic Teaching Resources

Name _____

Spelling Words	Class Words	My Words
hot cool		
cold wet		
warm dry		

Words

1. _____

   _____

   _____

2. _____

   _____

   _____

3. _____

   _____

4. _____

   _____

   _____

5. _____

   _____

6. _____

   _____

   _____

7. _____

   _____

   _____

8. _____

   _____

9. _____

   _____

   _____

10. _____

    _____

ABC Order

1. _____

2. _____

3. _____

4. _____

5. _____

6. _____

7. _____

8. _____

9. _____

10. _____

Word Boxes

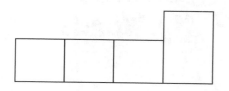 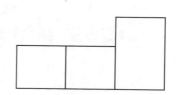 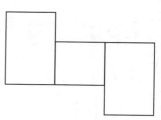

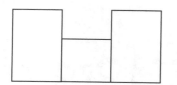  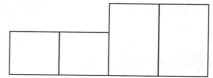

Sentences

1. Let's _____ the cold pizza before we eat it.

2. The weather was _____ and snowy.

3. After it rained it was very _____ outside.

4. The cookies had to _____ after they came out of the oven.

5. It was way too _____ last summer!

6. He likes to _____ off with a fluffy towel.

Bonus

1. _____

_____

2. _____

_____

Week-by-Week Homework Packets: Spelling Grade 1 Scholastic Teaching Resources

Name _____

Spelling Words	Class Words	My Words
mother sister		
father girl		
brother boy		

Words

1. _____

_____

_____

2. _____

_____

_____

3. _____

_____

_____

4. _____

_____

_____

5. _____

_____

6. _____

_____

_____

7. _____

_____

_____

8. _____

_____

_____

9. _____

_____

_____

10. _____

_____

_____

A B C Order

1. _____

2. _____

3. _____

4. _____

5. _____

6. _____

7. _____

8. _____

9. _____

10. _____

Word Boxes

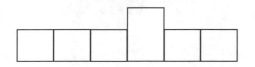 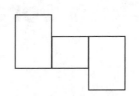 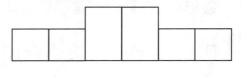

 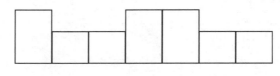 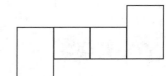

Sentences

1. Her _____ has a beard.

2. My _____ will pick us up at four o'clock.

3. I saw your _____ and his friends at the park.

4. Kevin is a friendly _____.

5. My _____ left her backpack at school.

6. There is a new _____ in our class.

Bonus

1. _____

_____

2. _____

_____

Week-by-Week Homework Packets: Spelling Grade 1 Scholastic Teaching Resources

Name _____

Spelling Words

school	house
garden	farm
flower	grass

Class Words

My Words

Words

1. _____

_____

_____

2. _____

_____

_____

3. _____

_____

_____

4. _____

_____

_____

5. _____

_____

6. _____

_____

_____

7. _____

_____

_____

8. _____

_____

_____

9. _____

_____

_____

10. _____

_____

_____

ABC Order

1. _____

2. _____

3. _____

4. _____

5. _____

6. _____

7. _____

8. _____

9. _____

10. _____

Word Boxes

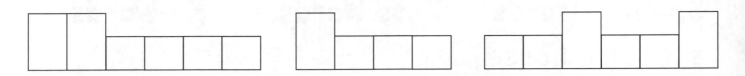

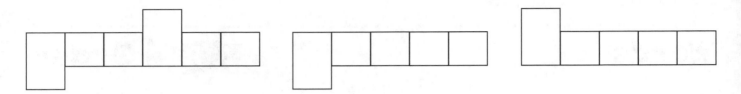

Sentences

1. My dad cuts the _____ with a lawn mower.

2. He grows many vegetables in his _____.

3. They have a _____ with lots of animals.

4. She lives in a brick _____.

5. A beautiful _____ grew in my garden.

6. What is the name of your _____?

Bonus

1. _____

_____

2. _____

_____

Week-by-Week Homework Packets: Spelling Grade 1   Scholastic Teaching Resources

Name _____

Spelling Words | Class Words | My Words

Spelling Words	
cat	duck
horse	dog
cow	frog

Words

1. _____

_____

_____

2. _____

_____

_____

3. _____

_____

_____

4. _____

_____

_____

5. _____

_____

6. _____

_____

7. _____

_____

8. _____

_____

9. _____

_____

10. _____

_____

A B C Order

1. _____

2. _____

3. _____

4. _____

5. _____

6. _____

7. _____

8. _____

9. _____

10. _____

Word Boxes

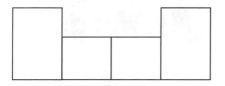

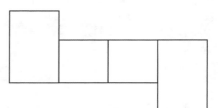

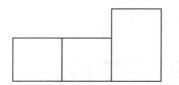
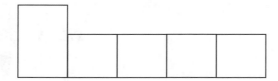
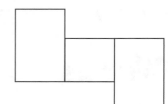

Sentences

1. That _____ has a loud bark!

2. I would like to learn how to ride a _____.

3. The mother _____ was sitting on her eggs.

4. We caught a big _____ near the pond.

5. I saw a _____ being milked.

6. My _____ has fluffy fur.

Bonus

1. _____

   _____

2. _____

   _____

Week-by-Week Homework Packets: Spelling Grade 1 Scholastic Teaching Resources

Name _____

Spelling Words | Class Words | My Words

rabbit   pig

sheep   fish

bird   goat

Words

1. _____

_____

_____

2. _____

_____

_____

3. _____

_____

_____

4. _____

_____

5. _____

_____

6. _____

_____

_____

7. _____

_____

_____

8. _____

_____

_____

9. _____

_____

10. _____

_____

ABC Order

1. _____

2. _____

3. _____

4. _____

5. _____

6. _____

7. _____

8. _____

9. _____

10. _____

Word Boxes

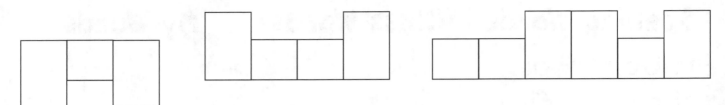

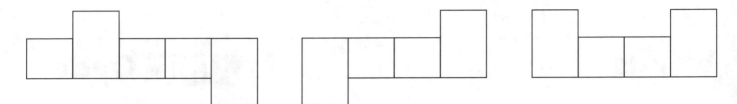

Sentences

1. Did you see that _____ fly by?

2. My pet _____ has floppy ears.

3. I saw the yellow and orange _____ in the lake.

4. The baby _____ has a curly tail.

5. A _____ can be called a lamb when it is young.

6. A baby _____ is called a kid.

Bonus

1. _____

_____

2. _____

_____

Week-by-Week Homework Packets: Spelling Grade 1 Scholastic Teaching Resources

Name _____

Spelling Words	Class Words	My Words
purple red yellow blue green color		

Words

1. _____

_____

_____

2. _____

_____

_____

3. _____

_____

_____

4. _____

_____

_____

5. _____

_____

6. _____

_____

_____

7. _____

_____

_____

8. _____

_____

_____

9. _____

_____

_____

10. _____

_____

A B C Order

1. _____

2. _____

3. _____

4. _____

5. _____

6. _____

7. _____

8. _____

9. _____

10. _____

Word Boxes

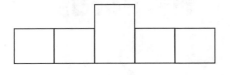
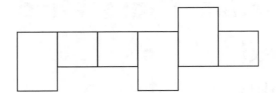
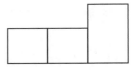

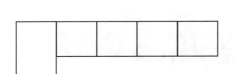
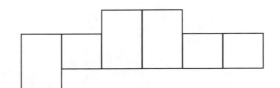
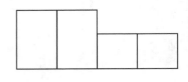

Sentences

1. The _____ rose smelled beautiful.

2. The sky was clear and _____.

3. He slipped on a _____ banana.

4. What is your favorite _____?

5. I love to eat _____ beans.

6. The girls both have _____ coats.

Bonus

1. _____

   _____

2. _____

   _____

70

Name _____

Spelling Words

orange	pink
black	gray
brown	white

Class Words

My Words

Words

1. _____

_____

_____

2. _____

_____

_____

3. _____

_____

_____

4. _____

_____

_____

5. _____

_____

6. _____

_____

_____

7. _____

_____

_____

8. _____

_____

_____

9. _____

_____

_____

10. _____

_____

ABC Order

1. _____

2. _____

3. _____

4. _____

5. _____

6. _____

7. _____

8. _____

9. _____

10. _____

Word Boxes

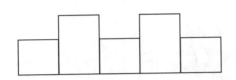
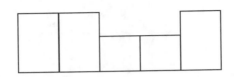
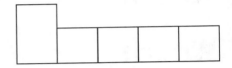

Sentences

1. A puff of _____ smoke came from the chimney.

2. The snow was cold and _____.

3. The baby girl wore a _____ dress.

4. The tires on the bus are _____.

5. There was a _____ mouse in my house!

6. He ate an _____ for his snack.

Bonus

1. _____

_____

2. _____

_____

Name _____

REVIEW
Spelling Work

☐ **Monday**   Word Search: Find your review words in the word search and circle them.

☐ **Tuesday**   Word Scramble: Unscramble your review words and write them on the blank lines.

☐ **Wednesday**   Review Words: Read all of your review words from your word list. Ask a family member or friend to listen while you spell each word. Be sure to spell each word correctly!

☐ **Thursday**   Sentences: Write five sentences. In each sentence use as many review words as you can. Underline your review words in each sentence.

☐ **Friday**   Return this homework.

Parent Signature _____

Name _____

Word Search

Word Bank

I	the
and	you
with	her
that	he
a	as
on	by
are	have
from	

```
t  h  e  o  g  n  p  d  h  t
h  b  m  I  a  n  d  c  e  q
a  r  e  s  y  w  f  m  r  y
t  a  s  f  h  a  v  e  z  o
z  t  v  a  j  c  k  g  x  u
w  i  t  h  b  h  f  r  o  m
b  c  q  k  y  e  i  d  n  u
```

Word Scramble

Word Bank

in	for	but	at	one
she	was	they	be	to
or	is	of	it	his

rof _____

ot _____

fo _____

sih _____

si _____

seh _____

neo _____

swa _____

tbu _____

hyet _____

ti _____

ni _____

ro _____

eb _____

ta _____

Review Words

a	I
to	the
and	you
is	it
of	in
for	that
on	as
he	she
are	was
at	be
his	her
with	they
or	by
one	have
but	from

Week-by-Week Homework Packets: Spelling Grade 1 Scholastic Teaching Resources

Name _____

Word Search

Word Bank

go	me
no	can
had	when
there	which
my	how
each	them
make	were
good	

```
k g o s t w p l w g
t h e m x e a c h o
w b v m y r d z e o
h f h l k e c a n d
i r a m a k e n y n
c o d r q d u o t h
h i u g m e p w j o
t h e r e l i a c w
```

Word Scramble

Word Bank

all	we	an	not	what
this	your	said	about	up
do	him	will	like	if

fi _____   mhi _____

ikle _____   od _____

ont _____   ew _____

na _____   lal _____

stih _____   pu _____

thaw _____

lilw _____

ryuo _____

dais _____

botua _____

Review Words

go	no
all	had
what	this
me	we
can	not
your	when
if	an
my	said
which	there
up	how
will	each
like	them
do	him
were	make
good	about

Name _____

Word Search

Word Bank

has	two
many	then
into	more
than	other
now	use
been	look
down	three
people	

```
a r p c i j d o w n
u s e t n m a n y z
o z o h t o k j t b
n h p e o t h r e e
t a l n q h d t f e
h s e w v e u w e n
a x c m o r e o i m
n o w l b g l o o k
```

Word Scramble

Word Bank

so	out	see	under	their
some	these	would	did	who
way	time	find	first	could

enrdu _____

dinf _____

ese _____

yaw _____

os _____

itfrs _____

eitrh _____

loudw _____

docul _____

tseeh _____

ddi _____

ietm _____

owh _____

meso _____

tuo _____

Review Words

out	then
some	two
their	many
so	has
use	into
these	other
been	more
see	than
time	could
way	look
who	now
first	people
find	three
did	down
over	would

Name _____

Word Search

Word Bank

may	only
made	call
over	again
here	because
walk	done
best	come
going	very
think	

```
o p b e s t m p o v
v w m z f n h e r e
e q a c a l l p u r
r a d x g j k m a y
g b e c a u s e x b
o n l y i r q d t w
k t h i n k s o j a
l u d c o m e n e l
g o i n g s r e m k
```

Word Scramble

Word Bank

day	say	get	man	water
thing	long	part	back	woman
stop	know	must	just	after

ujst _____

gonl _____

ospt _____

ays _____

utms _____

trewa _____

cbka _____

mnowa _____

intgh _____

ftrae _____

tge _____

rapt _____

nma _____

ownk _____

yda _____

Review Words

only	day
made	water
may	get
long	call
man	stop
over	because
again	thing
here	say
come	after
going	back
walk	part
done	woman
best	know
think	must
very	just

Name _____

Word Search

Word Bank

why	tall
does	give
away	right
much	little
far	dry
boy	cold
cool	sister
father	

```
c s w z d b g i v e
o t h l o y p s f d
o p y i e z a w a y
l k c t s h x u t n
m f o t l r i g h t
t a l l y v c b e a
n r d e x f r d r y
g a u q m u c h l s
s i s t e r p b o y
```

Word Scramble

Word Bank

put	girl	most	thank	left
short	never	children	hot	wet
warm	where	brother	mother	birthday

antkh _____   ewt _____

omts _____   marw _____

oth _____   veern _____

fetl _____   rigl _____

orths _____   utp _____

ydtirbha _____

omreht _____

orbethr _____

idenrlhc _____

ewerh _____

Review Words

away	little
most	right
thank	where
much	put
why	tall
never	children
does	far
give	short
left	birthday
girl	boy
sister	father
brother	mother
hot	dry
wet	warm
cool	cold

Name _____

Word Search

Word Bank

farm	cat
cow	fish
bird	horse
school	flower
gray	red
white	brown
rabbit	yellow
purple	

```
n c o w h q b i r d
s v m n f a r m a t
p u r p l e o e b w
g c a t o s w s b h
r l h k w x n c i i
a k o j e c f h t t
y p r x r e d o g e
f i s h o b k o y n
e w e g y e l l o w
```

Word Scramble

Word Bank

dog	pig	duck	frog	grass
house	sheep	garden	goat	blue
pink	color	green	black	orange

ablkc _____

negre _____

eepsh _____

grfo _____

aogt _____

nroaeg _____

sargs _____

orlco _____

daergn _____

ouseh _____

ipkn _____

gpi _____

ulbe _____

ogd _____

cduk _____

Review Words

farm	grass
house	school
garden	flower
cat	dog
cow	duck
horse	frog
pig	bird
fish	goat
sheep	rabbit
red	blue
color	green
purple	yellow
pink	gray
white	black
brown	orange

Sentences

1. _____

_____

_____

2. _____

_____

_____

3. _____

_____

_____

4. _____

_____

_____

5. _____

_____

_____